HOLIDAY HISTORY
HALLOWEEN

by Kristine Spanier, MLIS

pogo

Ideas for Parents and Teachers

Pogo Books let children practice reading informational text while introducing them to nonfiction features such as headings, labels, sidebars, maps, and diagrams, as well as a table of contents, glossary, and index.

Carefully leveled text with a strong photo match offers early fluent readers the support they need to succeed.

Before Reading

- "Walk" through the book and point out the various nonfiction features. Ask the student what purpose each feature serves.
- Look at the glossary together. Read and discuss the words.

Read the Book

- Have the child read the book independently.
- Invite him or her to list questions that arise from reading.

After Reading

- Discuss the child's questions. Talk about how he or she might find answers to those questions.
- Prompt the child to think more. Ask: Did you know some Halloween traditions come from Ireland? Can you think of another holiday that comes from that country?

Pogo Books are published by Jump!
5357 Penn Avenue South
Minneapolis, MN 55419
www.jumplibrary.com

Copyright © 2023 Jump!
International copyright reserved in all countries. No part of this book may be reproduced in any form without written permission from the publisher.

Library of Congress Cataloging-in-Publication Data

Names: Spanier, Kristine, author.
Title: Halloween / by Kristine Spanier.
Description: Minneapolis, MN: Jump!, Inc., 2023.
Series: Holiday history | Includes index.
Audience: Ages 7-10
Identifiers: LCCN 2022014816 (print)
LCCN 2022014817 (ebook)
ISBN 9798885241281 (hardcover)
ISBN 9798885241298 (paperback)
ISBN 9798885241304 (ebook)
Subjects: LCSH: Halloween—Juvenile literature.
Classification: LCC GT4965 .S64 2023 (print)
LCC GT4965 (ebook)
DDC 394.2646—dc23/eng/20220328
LC record available at https://lccn.loc.gov/2022014816
LC ebook record available at https://lccn.loc.gov/2022014817

Editor: Eliza Leahy
Designer: Molly Ballanger

Photo Credits: Shutterstock, cover; GOLFX/Shutterstock, 1; JeniFoto/Shutterstock, 3; Ronny Enzenberg/Shutterstock, 4; Jaroslaw Grudzinski/Dreamstime, 5; North Wind Picture Archives/Alamy, 6-7; Anna Kucherova/Shutterstock, 8 (left); Yellowj/Shutterstock, 8 (right), 23 (bottom); Vintage Images/Alamy, 9; SolStock/iStock, 10-11; Harold M. Lambert/Getty, 12-13; RichVintage/iStock, 14-15; Hamiza Bakirci/Shutterstock, 16; Secretshutter/Stockimo/Alamy, 17; MERCURY studio/Shutterstock, 18-19; Stock Connection/SuperStock, 20-21; Viacheslav Lopatin/Shutterstock, 23 (top).

Printed in the United States of America at Corporate Graphics in North Mankato, Minnesota.

TABLE OF CONTENTS

CHAPTER 1
All Hallows' Evening...4

CHAPTER 2
Halloween Traditions..8

CHAPTER 3
Halloween Around the World.............................16

QUICK FACTS & TOOLS
Halloween Place of Origin....................................22
Quick Facts...22
Glossary..23
Index..24
To Learn More..24

CHAPTER 1

ALL HALLOWS' EVENING

Night comes early in fall. The air gets colder. Winds whistle. It can feel spooky. More than 2,000 years ago, people in Ireland and Scotland celebrated the **harvest** in fall. The event was called Samhain. People believed **spirits** might appear. They dressed in costumes to scare them away.

All Saints' Day is also in fall. It is November 1. It is a day to remember people who have died. It is a **Christian** holiday. Another name for it is All Hallows' Day. The night before is October 31. It is All Hallows' Evening.

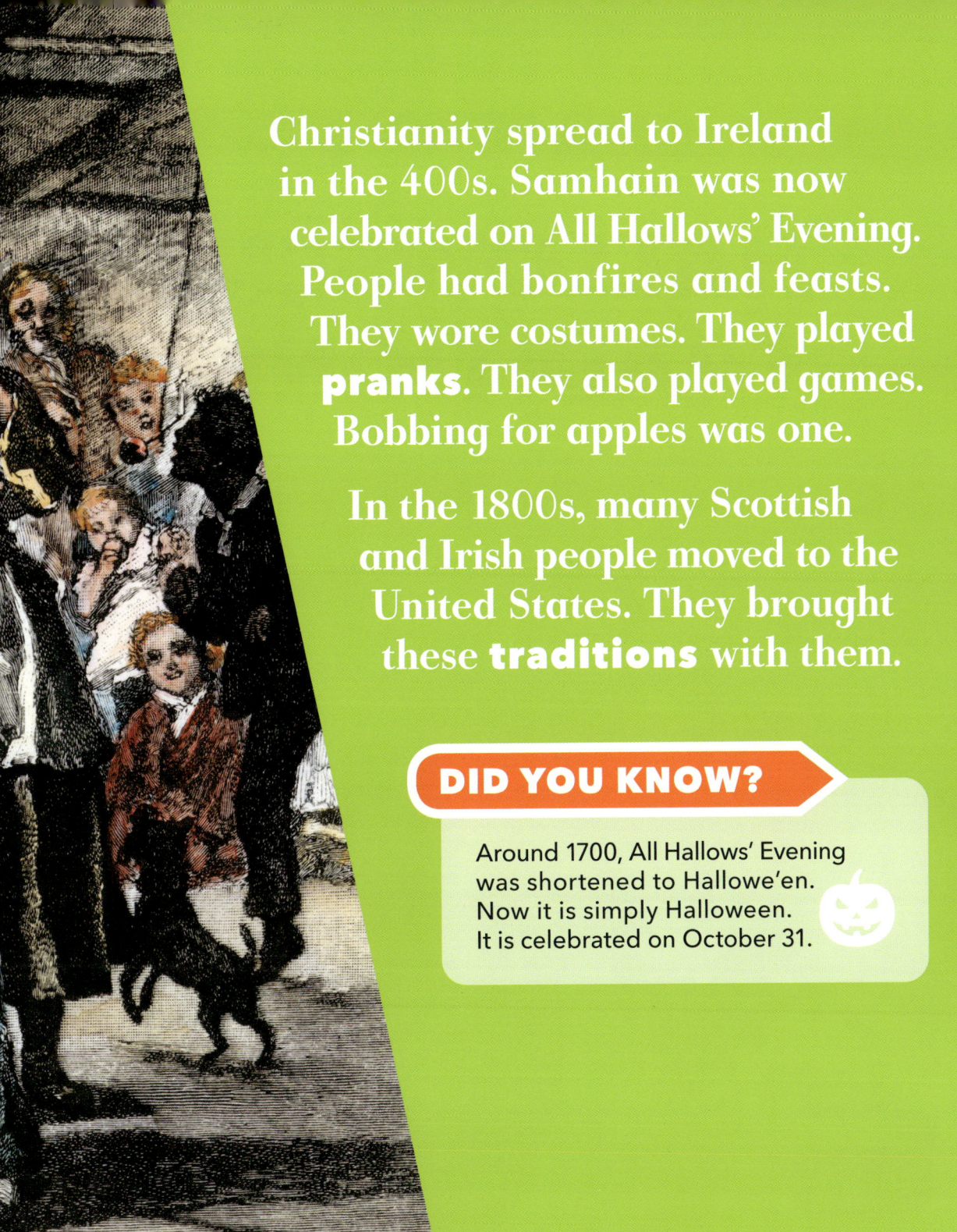

Christianity spread to Ireland in the 400s. Samhain was now celebrated on All Hallows' Evening. People had bonfires and feasts. They wore costumes. They played **pranks**. They also played games. Bobbing for apples was one.

In the 1800s, many Scottish and Irish people moved to the United States. They brought these **traditions** with them.

DID YOU KNOW?

Around 1700, All Hallows' Evening was shortened to Hallowe'en. Now it is simply Halloween. It is celebrated on October 31.

CHAPTER 2
HALLOWEEN TRADITIONS

One Irish **tale** is about Jack. He carried a **lantern** carved from a turnip. On Halloween, people in Ireland made their own turnip lanterns. They were called jack-o'-lanterns. When the Irish came to the United States, they used pumpkins. Pumpkins are much easier to carve.

turnip

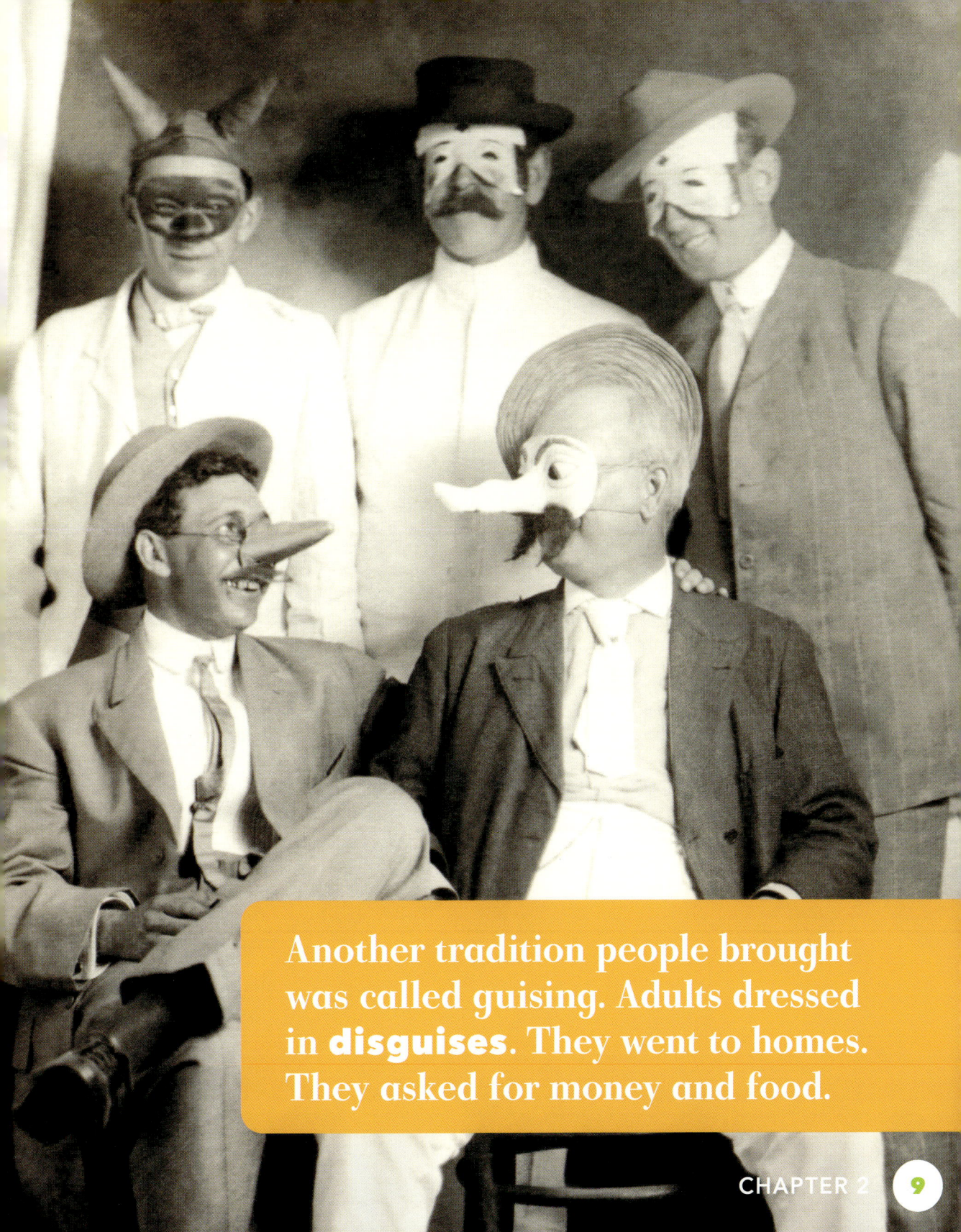

Another tradition people brought was called guising. Adults dressed in **disguises**. They went to homes. They asked for money and food.

CHAPTER 2

Pranks were common in the United States, too. But they got out of control.

City leaders decided to make Halloween a day for children. They held parades. Parents hosted parties.

Children were encouraged to trick-or-treat. Some began going door-to-door for candy and other treats in the 1930s. By the 1950s, kids across the United States did this every Halloween.

> **WHAT DO YOU THINK?**
>
> During World War II (1939–1945), sugar was limited. Many people did not have candy to give out. What do you think they could have given out instead?

CHAPTER 2

People used to only wear scary costumes on Halloween. As more children celebrated, fun costumes became common. But some kids still like to look scary!

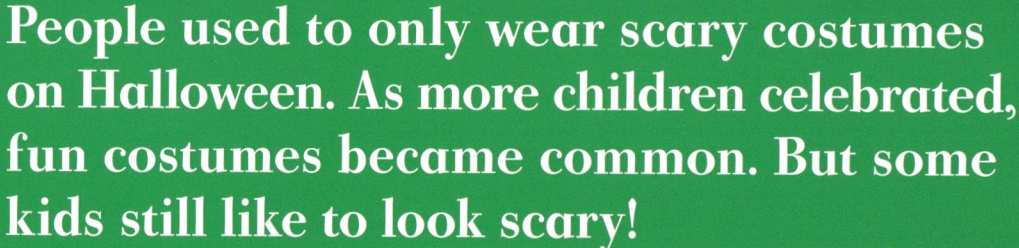

14 CHAPTER 2

TAKE A LOOK!

Orange, black, purple, and green are common Halloween colors. Take a look at other **symbols** of the holiday!

SPIDERWEB
BLACK CAT
SPIDER
WITCH
GHOST
JACK-O'-LANTERN
SKELETON
BAT
CANDY CORN
HAUNTED HOUSE

CHAPTER 2

CHAPTER 3
HALLOWEEN AROUND THE WORLD

Halloween has been celebrated in Sweden since the 1990s. Pumpkins are grown just for the holiday! Children dress up. They go to parties. They trick-or-treat.

pumpkin patch

People still celebrate Halloween in Ireland. Kids trick-or-treat. Families have bonfires. They play games. Barmbrack bread is a fruitcake with a toy baked inside. Whoever gets the toy may have good luck!

bonfire

CHAPTER 3

Adults in many parts of the world also like to dress up and go to parties. In South Korea, some go to **theme parks** with scary decorations. Others watch parades.

WHAT DO YOU THINK?

People move from one place to another. This is one way traditions spread. How else do you think traditions spread?

Haunted houses are popular on Halloween. So are haunted hayrides. People like to make their homes look spooky, too.

This holiday gives people a safe way to feel afraid. Some think it is fun! Do you like to be scared on Halloween?

CHAPTER 3

QUICK FACTS & TOOLS

HALLOWEEN PLACE OF ORIGIN

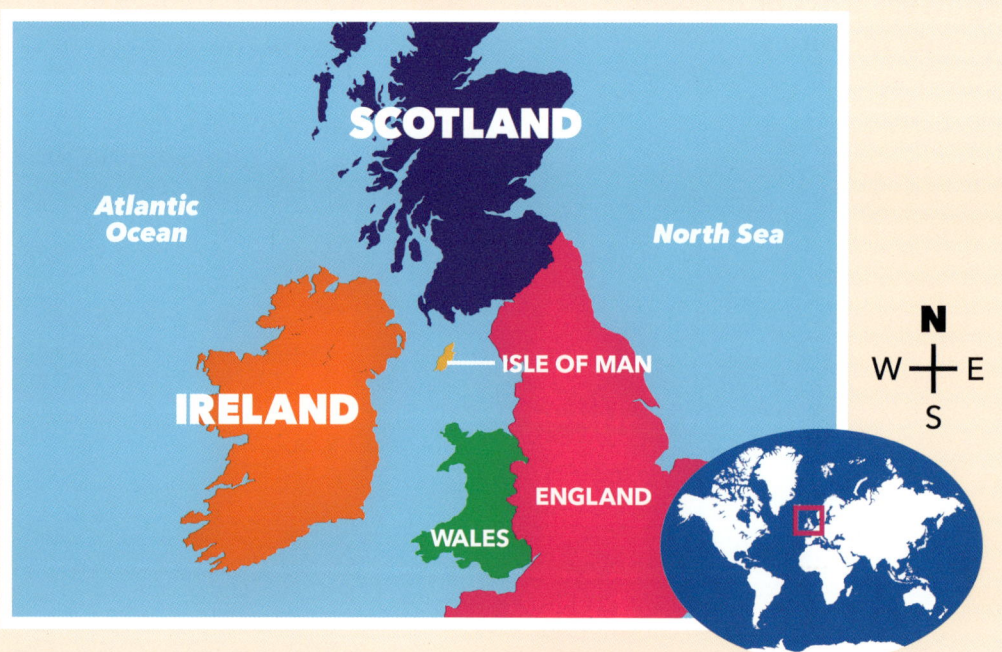

QUICK FACTS

Date: October 31

Places of Origin: Ireland and Scotland

Common Symbols: black cats, pumpkins, bats, ghosts, skeletons, spiders, witches

Foods: candy, caramel apples, pumpkin seeds

Traditions: dressing in costumes, trick-or-treating, parties, parades

GLOSSARY

Christian: Of or relating to Jesus or the religion based on his teachings.

disguises: Ways of dressing that hide identities.

harvest: The gathering of crops that are ready to eat.

haunted: To be inhabited by or visited by a ghost.

lantern: A kind of lamp.

pranks: Playful or mischievous tricks.

spirits: Ghosts or supernatural beings.

symbols: Objects or designs that stand for, suggest, or represent something else.

tale: A story about exciting and imaginary events.

theme parks: Parks with rides and attractions based on particular subjects.

traditions: Customs, ideas, or beliefs that are handed down from one generation to the next.

INDEX

All Hallows' Evening 5, 7
All Saints' Day 5
barmbrack bread 17
bonfires 7, 17
candy 12, 15
costumes 4, 7, 14
fall 4, 5
feasts 7
games 7, 17
guising 9
harvest 4
haunted houses 15, 20
Ireland 4, 7, 8, 17
jack-o'-lanterns 8, 15
parades 11, 19
parties 11, 16, 19
pranks 7, 11
pumpkins 8, 16
Samhain 4, 7
Scotland 4, 7
South Korea 19
spirits 4
Sweden 16
symbols 15
trick-or-treat 12, 16, 17
United States 7, 8, 11, 12

TO LEARN MORE

Finding more information is as easy as 1, 2, 3.

1. Go to www.factsurfer.com
2. Enter "Halloween" into the search box.
3. Choose your book to see a list of websites.

QUICK FACTS & TOOLS